Patrick Heron Gouaches from 1961 to 1996

X

SIGN

D1465317

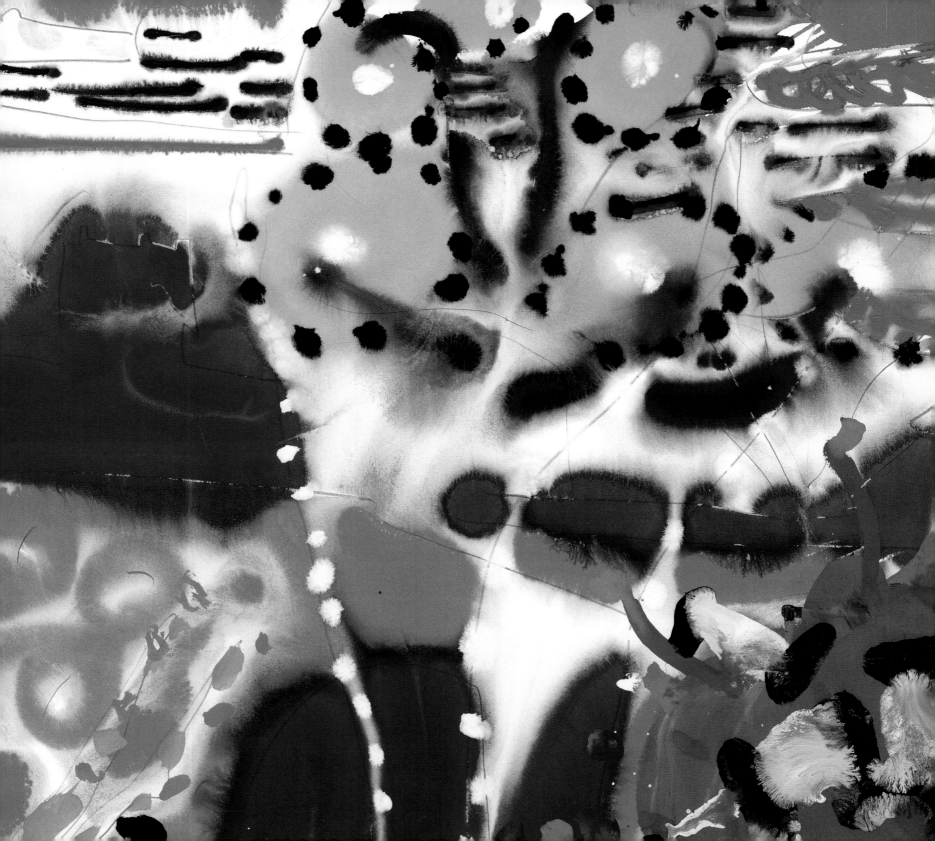

Patrick Heron Gouaches from 1961 to 1996

Waddington Galleries

9 February – 12 March 2005

'A Note on My Gouaches'

written to accompany an exhibition of Heron's gouaches at the Caledonian Club, Edinburgh, 1985

My gouaches are not a substitute for the oil paintings. Nor are they preliminary sketches, or means for trying out new colour-shapes or configurations of dovetailed colour-shapes to feature in later paintings on canvas. They are works in their own right; and their quality, in fact, doesn't even overlap with the canvases' in many respects. Or so I feel.

A painting has a certain identifiable speed of execution, which it communicates. You can feel the exact speed of Van Gogh's painting hand, as your eye skips across the staccato-surfaces of jabbed, separate strokes of that square-tipped brush of his. You can also physically identify with the extremely swift and broad scribble-action in Matisse; the gliding brush whose speed changes every second as it makes the painting.

In my gouaches, the tempo is dictated, quite apart from the particular needs of the area-shapes I make, by the nature of the wet medium itself. I like the water in the paint mixture to lead me; to suggest the scribbled drawing which gives birth to the images.

My gouaches have always had this fast-moving fluidity of drawing, and a softness, coming from the watery medium itself, which the oil paintings cannot share. Throughout the 1970s, in fact, my gouaches and my oil paintings occupied very different departments in the field of pictorial experience. The canvases had to have a certain degree of rigidity, by comparison. It is only recently, in the development shown in my large (and small) canvases since 1981, [...] that an *apparently* more rough and ragged paint application brings the canvases more into line with that quality of fluent, fluid colour which has been a characteristic of the gouaches for a very long time.

1

Hard Disc, Soft Square (Coffee Ochre) : February 1961

gouache on paper
22 $\frac{1}{8}$ × 30 $\frac{3}{8}$ in / 56.2 × 77.1 cm

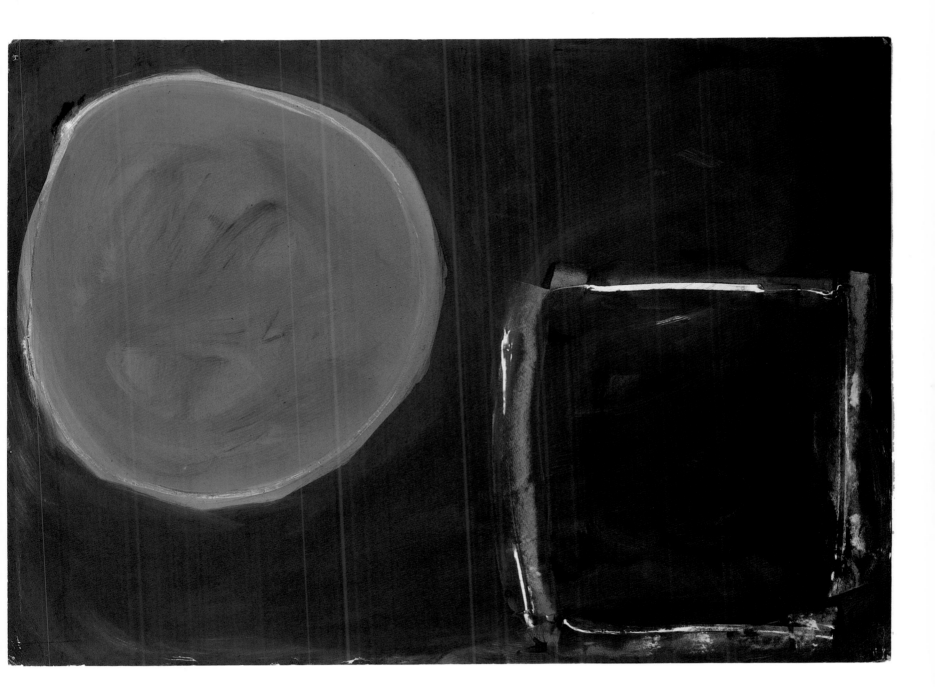

2

Bright Rectangles : 1963

gouache on paper
22 $\frac{1}{8}$ × 30 $\frac{1}{4}$ in / 56.2 × 76.8 cm

3

Concentric Rings : 1963

gouache on paper
15 $\frac{1}{4}$ × 22 $\frac{1}{4}$ in / 38.7 × 56.5 cm

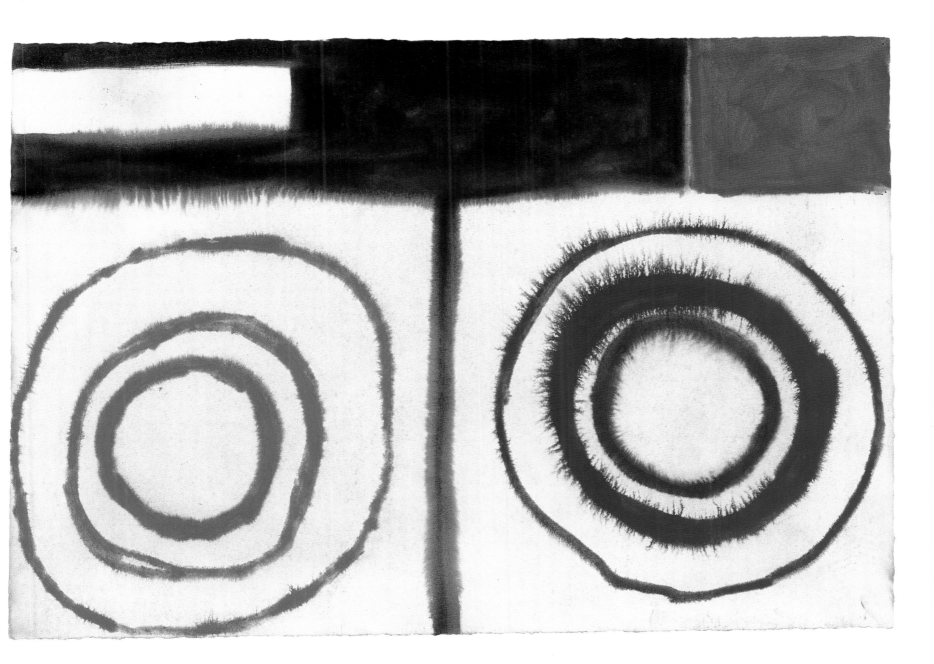

4

Blue Disc Flooding : June 1964

gouache on paper
22 ⅞ × 31 in / 58.1 × 78.7 cm

5

Mysterious Grey : November 23 : 1964

gouache on paper
17 $^5/_8$ × 27 $^1/_2$ in / 44.8 × 70 cm

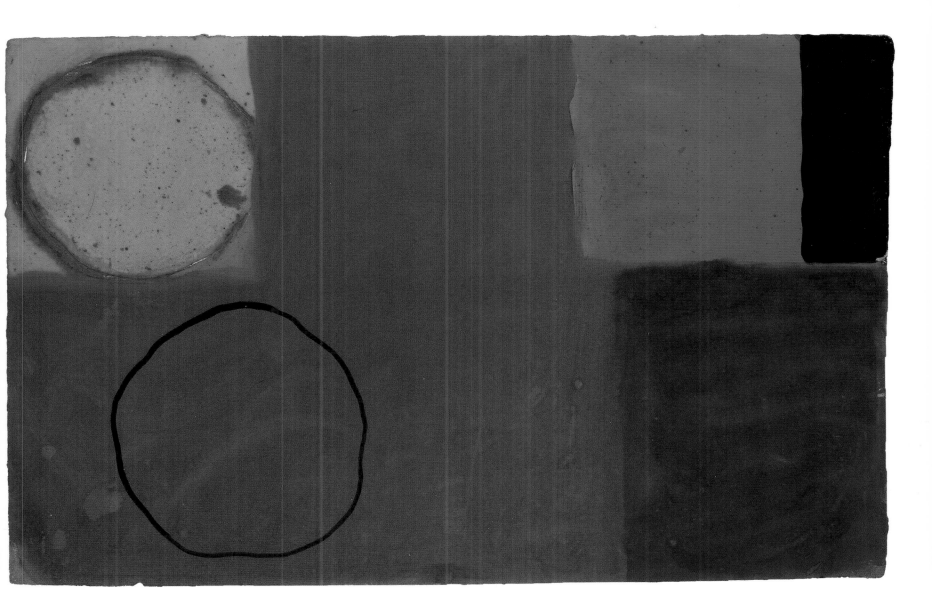

Complex Yellows : February 1966

gouache on paper
22 $\frac{1}{2}$ × 30 $\frac{5}{8}$ in / 57 × 77.9 cm

7

Yellows, Reds and Violet : December 1966

gouache on paper
22 $\frac{1}{2}$ × 30 $\frac{7}{8}$ in / 57.2 × 78.3 cm

8

Lemon in Plum, Orange in Pink : December 1966

gouache on paper
15 ³/₈ × 22 ¹/₂ in / 39 × 57.1 cm

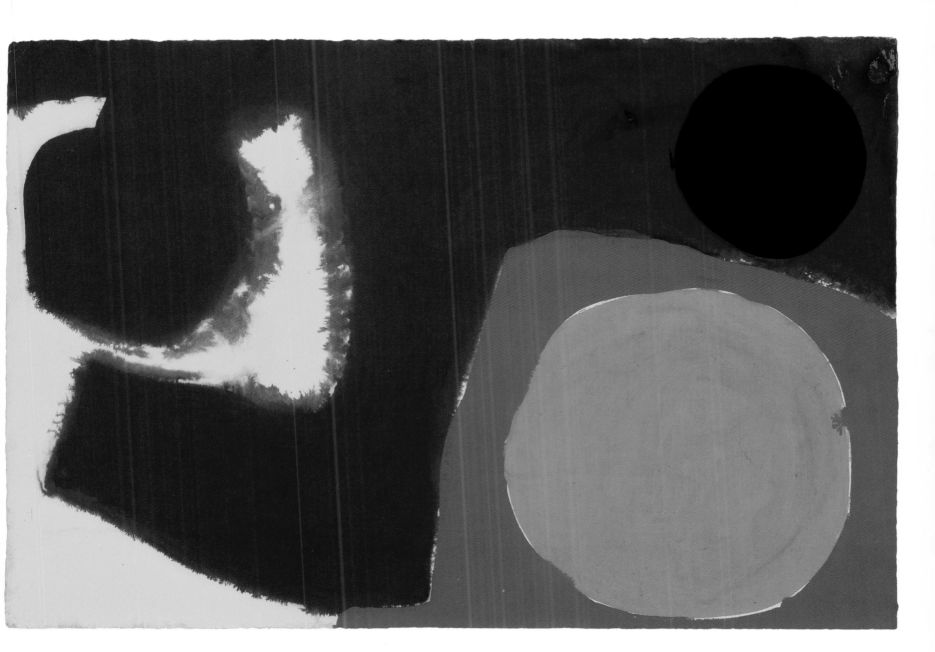

9

Scarlet, Dark Blue and Lemon to Right of Cobalt : April 1968

gouache on paper
22 ¹/₂ × 31 in / 57.1 × 78.7 cm

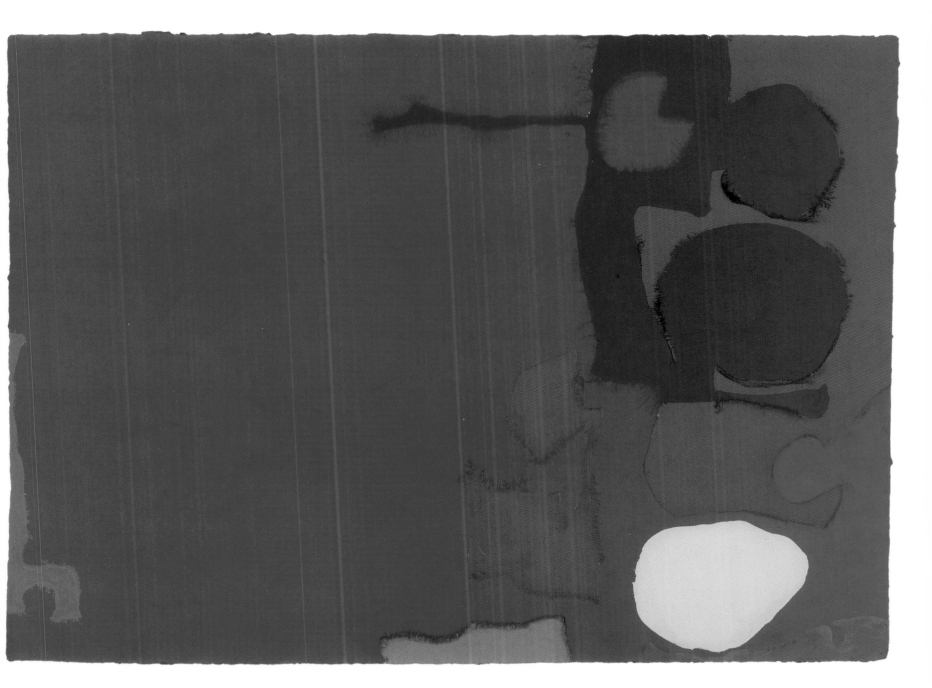

Four Square Complex (Reds with Lemon) : May 1968

gouache on paper
23 $\frac{1}{4}$ × 30 $\frac{3}{4}$ in / 59 × 78 cm

March : 1980

gouache on paper
22 $\frac{1}{2}$ × 30 $\frac{3}{4}$ in / 57 × 78 cm

April 25 : 1986

gouache on paper
17 $\frac{1}{2}$ × 27 $\frac{1}{4}$ in / 44.4 × 69 cm

13

May 9 : 1986

gouache on paper
12 $^{7}/_{8}$ × 18 $^{5}/_{8}$ in / 32.7 × 47.3 cm

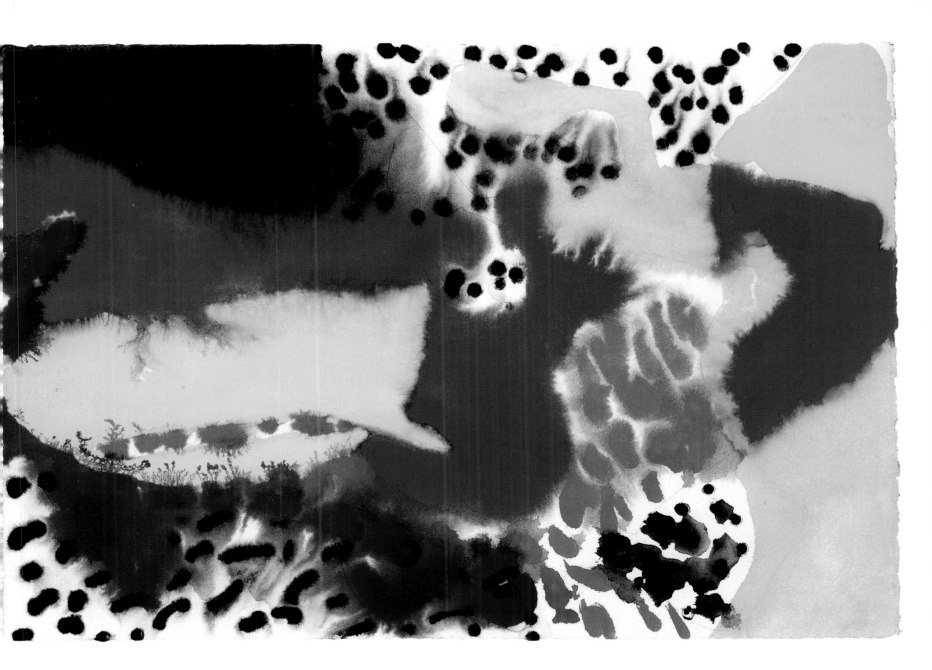

14

May 11 : 1986 : II

gouache on paper
12 ¾ × 18 ¾ in / 32.5 × 47.5 cm

15

January 22 : 1989

gouache on paper
22 $^5/_8$ × 31 $^1/_8$ in / 57.5 × 79.1 cm

Sydney : November 11 : 1989

gouache on paper
23 × 30 in / 58.4 × 76.2 cm

27 February : 1995 : II

gouache on paper
13 $^{3}/_{4}$ × 19 $^{7}/_{8}$ in / 34.9 × 50.5 cm

18

30 June : 1995

gouache on paper
22 $^{3}/_{4}$ × 30 $^{1}/_{2}$ in / 57.8 × 77.5 cm

19

2 July : 1995 : I

gouache on paper
22 $^5/_8$ × 30 $^3/_8$ in / 57.4 × 77 cm

20

28 October : 1996

gouache on paper
12 $\frac{1}{4}$ × 16 $\frac{1}{8}$ in / 30.9 × 40.9 cm

List of Works

Biography

List of Works

1

Hard Disc, Soft Square (Coffee Ochre) : February 1961
gouache on paper
22 $^1/_8$ × 30 $^3/_8$ in / 56.2 × 77.1 cm

signed and titled on reverse 'PATRICK HERON' 'HARD DISC, SOFT SQUARE (COFFEE OCHRE) : FEBRUARY 1961'

Provenance
Patrick Heron

Exhibited
'13 Brittiska Konstnärer', organised by the Riksförbundet för bildande konst, Moderna Museet, Stockholm; touring Sweden, 1961–1962, catalogue no.28 (not repro.)
'Patrick Heron: Gouaches 1961–1989', Waddington Galleries, London, 26 April – 20 May 1989, catalogue no.2 (repro. in colour p.9)

Literature
'Patrick Heron: Works from 1956 to 1969', Waddington Galleries, London, 2002, catalogue no.26 (repro. in colour p.42) (not exhibited)

2

Bright Rectangles : 1963
gouache on paper
22 $^1/_8$ × 30 $^1/_4$ in / 56.2 × 76.8 cm

signed and titled on reverse 'PATRICK HERON' 'BRIGHT RECTANGLES : 1963'

Provenance
Patrick Heron
The artist's family

Literature
'Patrick Heron: Works from 1956 to 1969', Waddington Galleries, London, 2002, catalogue no.30 (repro. in colour p.46) (not exhibited)

3

Concentric Rings : 1963
gouache on paper
15 $^1/_4$ × 22 $^1/_4$ in / 38.7 × 56.5 cm

signed and dated on reverse 'Patrick Heron' 'September 1963'

Provenance
Patrick Heron
The artist's family

Exhibited
'Patrick Heron', The Waddington Galleries, London, 24 November – 19 December 1964, catalogue no.27 (not repro.)
'Paintings by Patrick Heron and Bryan Wynter', organised by Richard Demarco, Hume Tower, Edinburgh, 30 August – 11 September 1965, catalogue no.9 (not repro.)

4

Blue Disc Flooding : June 1964
gouache on paper
22 $^7/_8$ × 31 in / 58.1 × 78.7 cm

signed and titled on reverse 'Patrick Heron' 'Blue Disc Flooding : June 1964'

Provenance
Patrick Heron
Kasmin Gallery, London

Exhibited
'Patrick Heron', The Waddington Galleries, London, 24 November – 19 December 1964, catalogue no.24 (not repro.)
'Drawings by Eleven British Artists', organised by South West Arts Association and Arnolfini, Bristol; touring to Strode Theatre, Street, Somerset; Queen's Hall, Barnstaple, Devon; The Beaford Centre, Winkleigh, Devon; Weymouth Arts Centre, Weymouth, Dorset; Bridgwater Arts Centre, Bridgwater, Somerset; College of St Matthias, Bristol; Falmouth Arts Centre, Falmouth, Cornwall, 15 January – 31 August 1968, catalogue no.16 (not repro.)

5

Mysterious Grey : November 23 : 1964
gouache on paper
17 $^5/_8$ × 27 $^1/_2$ in / 44.8 × 70 cm

signed and titled on reverse 'PATRICK HERON' 'MYSTERIOUS GREY : NOVEMBER 23 : 1964'

Provenance
Patrick Heron
The artist's family

Literature
'Patrick Heron', Mel Gooding, Phaidon Press, London, 1994, p.176 (repro. in colour p.178)

6

Complex Yellows : February 1966
gouache on paper
22 $^1/_2$ × 30 $^5/_8$ in / 57 × 77.9 cm

signed and titled on reverse 'Patrick Heron' 'COMPLEX YELLOWS : FEBRUARY 1966'

Provenance
Patrick Heron
Waddington Galleries, London
Private Collection, London

Exhibited
'Patrick Heron/Ceri Richards', Kunstnernes Hus, Oslo, 21 October – 12 November 1967, catalogue no.17 (not repro.)
'Patrick Heron', Bear Lane Gallery, Oxford, 4 May – 1 June 1968, catalogue no.2 (not repro.)

7

Yellows, Reds and Violet : December 1966
gouache on paper
22 ½ × 30 ⅞ in / 57.2 × 78.3 cm

signed and titled on reverse 'PATRICK HERON'
'YELLOWS, REDS AND VIOLET : DECEMBER 1966'

Provenance
Patrick Heron
The artist's family

Exhibited
'Patrick Heron', Bear Lane Gallery, Oxford, 4 May –
1 June 1968, catalogue no.6 (not repro.)
'Terry Frost et Patrick Heron', organised in
collaboration with The British Council, La Galerie le
Balcon des Arts, Paris, June – August 1977

8

Lemon in Plum, Orange in Pink : December 1966
gouache on paper
15 ⅜ × 22 ½ in / 39 × 57.1 cm

signed and titled on reverse 'PATRICK HERON'
'LEMON IN PLUM, ORANGE IN PINK : DECEMBER
1966'

Provenance
Patrick Heron
The artist's family

Exhibited
'Patrick Heron: Gouaches 1961 – 1989',
Waddington Galleries, London, 26 April – 20 May
1989, catalogue no.3 (not repro.)
'The Tenth Leeds Art Fair', Leeds Corn Exchange,
29 April – 1 May 1994 (repro. in colour on front
cover of catalogue)

Literature
'Patrick Heron: Works from 1956 to 1969',
Waddington Galleries, London, 2002, catalogue
no.31 (repro. in colour p.47) (not exhibited)

9

**Scarlet, Dark Blue and Lemon to Right of Cobalt :
April 1968**
gouache on paper
22 ½ × 31 in / 57.1 × 78.7 cm

signed and titled on reverse 'PATRICK HERON'
'SCARLET, DARK BLUE AND LEMON TO RIGHT OF
COBALT : APRIL 1968'

Provenance
Patrick Heron
The Waddington Galleries, London
Private Collection, New York (purchased from the
above in October 1969)
Private Collection, New York

Exhibited
'Patrick Heron: gouaches', The Waddington
Galleries, London, 2–27 July 1968

Literature
'Art and Artists', July 1968 (repro. in b&w p.51)

10

Four Square Complex (Reds with Lemon) : May 1968
gouache on paper
23 ¼ × 30 ¾ in / 59 × 78 cm

signed and titled on reverse 'PATRICK HERON' 'FOUR
SQUARE COMPLEX (REDS WITH LEMON) : MAY 1968'

Provenance
Patrick Heron
The artist's family

Exhibited
'Patrick Heron: gouaches', The Waddington
Galleries, London, 2–27 July 1968
'Patrick Heron from Eagles Nest: Paintings and
Drawing 1925–1985', Newlyn Art Gallery, 26
September – 26 October 1985, exhibition list no.27

11

March : 1980
gouache on paper
22 ½ × 30 ¾ in / 57 × 78 cm

signed and titled on reverse 'Patrick Heron'
'MARCH : 1980'

Provenance
Patrick Heron
The artist's family

12

April 25 : 1986
gouache on paper
17 ½ × 27 ¼ in / 44.4 × 69 cm

signed and titled on reverse 'Patrick Heron'
'APRIL 25 : 1986'

Provenance
Patrick Heron
The artist's family

13

May 9 : 1986
gouache on paper
12 ⅞ × 18 ⅝ in / 32.7 × 47.3 cm

signed and titled on reverse 'Patrick Heron'
'MAY 9 : 1986'

Provenance
Patrick Heron

Exhibited
'Patrick Heron – Jo Grimond Portraits and Garden
Gouaches', Waddington Galleries, London,
4–28 March 1987

14

May 11 : 1986 : II
gouache on paper
12 ¾ × 18 ¾ in / 32.5 × 47.5 cm

signed and titled on reverse 'Patrick Heron'
'MAY 11 : 1986 : II'

Provenance
Patrick Heron

15

January 22 : 1989
gouache on paper
22 ⅝ × 31 ⅛ in / 57.5 × 79.1 cm

signed and titled on the reverse 'Patrick Heron'
'JANUARY 22 : 1989'

Provenance
Patrick Heron
The artist's family

Exhibited
'Patrick Heron', Jersey Arts Centre, St. Helier,
Jersey, 11–28 April 1989

16

Sydney : November 11 : 1989
gouache on paper
23 × 30 in / 58.4 × 76.2 cm

titled on reverse 'SYDNEY : NOVEMBER 11 : 1989'

Provenance
Patrick Heron

Exhibited
'Patrick Heron: Gouaches', Waddington Galleries,
London, 7 May – 6 June 1998

A tapestry based on this gouache was made in 1993
by the Victorian Tapestry Workshop, Melbourne.
This tapestry was exhibited at the Victoria and Albert
Museum, London, in September 1993 and later at
the Australian High Commission, London, as part
of the exhibition 'The Stuff of Dreams: Masterworks
from the Victorian Tapestry Workshop' (see
'Australian Tapestries', Victorian Tapestry
Workshop, 1995, catalogue no.6, repro. in colour
pp.[28] & 29)

17

27 February : 1995 : II
gouache on paper
13 ¾ × 19 ⅞ in / 34.9 × 50.5 cm

signed and titled on reverse 'Patrick Heron'
'27 FEBRUARY 1995 : II'

Provenance
Patrick Heron

Exhibited
'Patrick Heron: recent gouaches', The Oxford
Gallery, Oxford, 27 March – 26 April 1995
Aldeburgh Festival, Suffolk, 15–26 June 1995
'Patrick Heron', Sligo Art Gallery, 15 August –
13 September 1996

18

30 June : 1995
gouache on paper
22 ¾ × 30 ½ in / 57.8 × 77.5 cm

signed and titled on reverse 'Patrick Heron'
'30 JUNE 1995'

Provenance
Patrick Heron

Exhibited
'Patrick Heron/Colin Lanceley', Sherman Galleries,
Paddington, Sydney, 24 August – 23 September
1995, catalogue no.22 (repro. in colour)
'Patrick Heron: Gouaches', Waddington Galleries,
London, 7 May – 6 June 1998

19

2 July : 1995 : I
gouache on paper
22 ⅝ × 30 ⅜ in / 57.4 × 77 cm

signed and titled on reverse 'Patrick Heron' '2 July :
1995 : I'

Provenance
Patrick Heron

Exhibited
'Patrick Heron/Colin Lanceley', Sherman Galleries,
Paddington, Sydney, 24 August – 23 September
1995, catalogue no.20 (repro. in colour)

20

28 October : 1996
gouache on paper
12 ¼ × 16 ⅛ in / 30.9 × 40.9 cm

signed and titled on reverse 'Patrick Heron'
'28 OCTOBER : 1996'

Provenance
Patrick Heron
The artist's family

Biography

1920 Born 30 January, Headingley, Leeds, son of Thomas Milner Heron and Eulalie 'Jack' Heron (née Davies)

1925 Lives near Newlyn, in Lelant and Zennor in West Cornwall. Tom Heron invited to become general manager of Crysede Silks, a firm owned by his friend Alec Walker

1927-28 The family spends five months at Eagles Nest, a house above Zennor which Heron was to buy in 1955

1928 The family moves to St Ives, above Porthmeor Beach. Tom Heron commissions the modernist architect Wells Coates to renovate existing shops for Crysede

1929 Tom Heron and Alec Walker part company and the family moves to Welwyn Garden City in Hertfordshire. Tom Heron founds Cresta Silks, and commissions Wells Coates to design the factory and shops and modernist artists to collaborate on packaging and design

1933 Patrick Heron visits the National Gallery in London for the first time and is shown the work of Cézanne by the art and craft teacher at his school, St George's, in Harpenden

1934 Commissioned by his father to make designs for Cresta Silks, and continues to design for the firm until 1951

1937–39 Attends Slade School of Fine Art, London, for two days a week. Meets Bryan Wynter

1940–43 Registers as a conscientious objector, and works on a chicken farm at Codicote, near Welwyn, and then as a labourer for Cambridgeshire War Agricultural Committee. Because of ill-health, he is exempted from further agricultural work

1941 Buys book illustrated with twenty-four paintings by Matisse chosen by the artist and published in 1939 by Braun et Cie

1943 Sees Matisse's *The Red Studio* at the Redfern Gallery, London

1944–45 Assistant at the Leach Pottery, St Ives (an approved work placement for a conscientious objector). Becomes friendly with a number of artists including Ben Nicholson, Barbara Hepworth, Naum Gabo, Adrian Stokes and Margaret Mellis

1945 Publishes his first piece of art criticism for *The New English Weekly*, which is on Ben Nicholson. Marries Delia Reiss in April and settles in Holland Park, London. He is now painting full-time

1946 Visits Braque exhibition at the Tate Gallery and writes an essay on the artist for *The New English Weekly*. Commissioned to give a series of radio talks on contemporary art for the newly-founded BBC Third Programme

1947 Appointed art critic of *The New Statesman and Nation* for which he continues to write until 1950. Birth of a daughter, Katharine. The family visit St Ives regularly, renting a cottage on the sea wall. First solo exhibition, at the Redfern Gallery, London

1948-49 Visits France, going first to the South and then to Paris where he sees the Salon de mai, visits Braque, and writes about young French painters. Birth of a daughter, Susanna

1949 Completes his portrait of T.S. Eliot, the first study for which was made in March 1947

1950 Paints a portrait of Sir Herbert Read

1951 First exhibition with the Penwith Society of Arts in Cornwall, St Ives. Continues his involvement with the Penwith Society until the late 1970s

1952 Retrospective exhibition of paintings and drawings opens at Wakefield City Art Gallery and travels to Leeds, Halifax, Scarborough, Nottingham and Hull. Visits Paris with William Scott to meet with French painters including De Staël and Soulages. Meets Japanese potter Shoji Hamada

1953 Visits Italy with his brother Giles and fellow artist Peter Lanyon. Begins teaching one day a week at Central School of Arts and Crafts, London, which he continues to do until 1956

1954 Meets the American art critic Clement Greenberg

1955 London correspondent for *Arts Digest*, New York (later *Arts*). Buys Eagles Nest, Zennor, Cornwall, and the family moves there in April 1956. A selection of his art criticism is published as *The Changing Forms of Art* in the UK, and in the USA the following year

1956 Exhibited *Tachiste Garden Paintings* at the Redfern Gallery, London

1957 'Stripe' paintings first exhibited in *Metavisual, Tachiste, Abstract*, a group exhibition at the Redfern Gallery (the title was found by Delia Heron)

1958 Takes over Ben Nicholson's studio at Porthmeor, St Ives, when Nicholson moves to Switzerland. Resigns as London correspondent of *Arts* (NY). Horizontal *Stripe Painting: November 1957–January 1958* installed in the London Offices of Percy Lund Humphries

1959 Awarded Grand Prize (International Jury) in Second John Moores Liverpool Exhibition, Walker Art Gallery

1960 First New York exhibition at Bertha Schaefer Gallery, and first solo exhibition at Waddington Galleries, London

1961 Pursuing their passionate commitment to conservation of the landscape, Patrick and Delia Heron buy moorland adjacent to Eagles Nest. Throughout his life, Heron engaged in many conservation issues, both in public and in print

1965 Awarded Silver Medal at VIII Bienal de São Paulo where he shares the British Pavilion with Victor Pasmore; lectures in São Paulo, Brasilia and Rio de Janeiro

1966 Publishes the first of a series of articles in *Studio International* in which he challenges the perceived supremacy of recent American art

1967 Visits Australia, lecturing in Perth and Sydney. A canoeing accident in Cornwall leaves him with a badly broken leg, as a result of which he works mostly in gouache for the next twelve months

1968 Retrospective exhibition opens in May at the Museum of Modern Art, Oxford

1970 In December resumes his polemic on the current perception of contemporary American art in a three hour lecture at the Institute of Contemporary Arts, London, entitled 'Symmetry in Painting: An Academic Formula'

1971 Publishes 'Murder of the Art Schools' in *The Guardian*, an article reflecting his long and active involvement in art education

1972 An exhibition of recent paintings and earlier canvases opens at The Whitechapel Art Gallery, London, in June

1973 'The Shape of Colour', a series of three talks he delivered as the 5th Power Lecture at the University of Sydney was also given in Brisbane, Canberra, Melbourne, Adelaide, Perth. Represents Great Britain at the first Sydney Biennale, in the Opera House

1974 In October, *The Guardian* publishes an article by Heron entitled 'The British Influence on the School of New York'. The article ran to 13,800 words

1978 Delivers 'The Colour of Colour', E. William Doty Lectures in Fine Arts, at the University of Texas at Austin, coinciding with a retrospective exhibition, *Paintings by Patrick Heron 1965–1977*, at the University art museum. Patrick and Delia Heron made honorary citizens of Texas by order of the Secretary of State for Texas. *The Shapes of Colour: 1943–1978*, a book of screenprints, published by Kelpra Editions, Waddington and Tooth Graphics

1979 Delia Heron dies on 3 May at Eagles Nest

1980 Appointed Trustee of the Tate Gallery, London, a position he holds until 1987

1982 Awarded Hon. D. Litt., by Exeter University

1983 Broadcast of *Patrick Heron*, BBC 'Omnibus' film, directed by Colin Nears, 13 March

1985 In July, a retrospective exhibition opens at the Barbican Art Gallery, City of London. *St Ives 1939–1964* opens at the Tate Gallery, London

1986 Awarded Hon. D. Litt., by University of Kent. Broadcast of *South Bank Show: Patrick Heron*, an LWT production, directed by John Read, 9 February

1987 Awarded Hon. Doctorate by Royal College of Art, London

1988 Visits Moscow and Leningrad on behalf of the Tate Gallery, London, with Director Alan Bowness and Richard Rogers, Chairman of the Trustees, in connection with a proposed exhibition of Matisse at the Tate Gallery

1989 Awarded Hon. Ph.D. by CNAA, Winchester School of Art. Visits Japan to give a lecture at the opening of 'St Ives' exhibition, Setagaya Art Museum, Tokyo. Makes a second visit to Moscow and Leningrad with Nicholas Serota on behalf of the Tate Gallery

1989–90 Takes up the position of Artist-in-Residence, Art Gallery of New South Wales, Sydney

1991 Visiting Artist, International Art Workshop, North Otago, New Zealand. Designs nine silk banners for Tate Gallery bookshop, London, refurbished by the architect John Miller

1992 Designs coloured glass window for Tate Gallery, St Ives (official opening June 1993). The artist works with Feary & Heron Architects and glass studio Wilhelm Derix GmbH and Co of Taunusstein, Germany. At the ime, the window is the largest unleaded glass window of its kind in the world. Peter Palumbo commissions Heron to design a kneeler to encircle Henry Moore's carved marble altarpiece at St Stephen Walbrook, London

1994 *Patrick Heron: Big Paintings* opens at the Camden Arts Centre, London, and travels to Arnolfini, Bristol. The monograph by Mel Gooding is published by Phaidon

1995 The National Portrait Gallery commissions a portrait of A.S. Byatt which is unveiled in 1998

1996 Created Honorary Fellow of Bretton Hall College, University of Leeds. *Patrick Heron on Art and Education* published by Bretton Hall, Wakefield. Exhibition of large paintings at Salander O'Reilly Galleries, New York

1996–98 'Big Painting Sculpture', Stag Place, Victoria, commissioned by Land Securities plc and carried out in collaboration with Feary & Heron Architects

1998 In June a major retrospective opens at the Tate Gallery selected by David Sylvester. Commissioned to make a series of etchings with Hugh Stoneman for Paragon Press entitled 'Brushworks'. *Painter as Critic*, selected writings edited by Mel Gooding is produced by Tate Publishing

1999 Dies on 20 March at his home in Zennor, Cornwall

The Directors of Waddington Galleries would like to express their
gratitude to Katharine and Susanna Heron and Julian Feary for
their generous help in organizing this exhibition

Patrick Heron Gouaches from 1961 to 1996

9 February – 12 March 2005

Waddington Galleries
11 Cork Street
London W1S 3LT

Telephone + 44 20 7851 2200 / 020 7851 2200
Facsimile + 44 20 7734 4146 / 020 7734 4146
mail@waddington-galleries.com
www.waddington-galleries.com

Monday to Friday 10am – 6pm
Saturday 10am – 1.30pm

Designed by Peter Campbell
Printed by Dexter Graphics
Photography by Prudence Cuming Associates

Published by Waddington Galleries

ISBN: 0-9548126-6-2

COVER:
January 22 : 1989 (detail) cat no. 15

FRONTISPIECE:
Sydney : November 11 : 1989 (detail) cat no. 16